USED WORLD

Other books by Gillian Conoley

WOMAN SPEAKING INSIDE FILM NOIR

SOME GANGSTER PAIN

TALL STRANGER

BECKON

LOVERS IN THE USED WORLD

POEMS BY
GILLIAN CONOLEY

CARNEGIE MELLON UNIVERSITY PRESS PITTSBURGH 2001

ACKNOWLEDGMENTS

Grateful acknowledgment is made to the editors of the following magazines and anthologies where these poems first appeared:

"The World," "Several Skylines," "Canon," "Turned Back," "The Extremes," "Childhood Home, a Panorama," "The First Three Minutes," "Careful," "Beauty and the Beast," "The Masters," "Fuck the Millenium," "The World," and "Date Movie" in *The American Poetry Review.*

"The Sky Drank In," "In the Wind that Unhands You," "The Violence" in *American Letters & Commentary.*

"The Splendor Fragments," "Flute Girl," "How Do I" in *New American Writing.*

"Lovers in the Used World" in *The Colorado Review.*

"Socrates," and "Alcibiades" in *Fence.*

"The World" in *Interim.*

"Three Women Then a Still Life" in *The Boston Review.*

"Training Films of the Real," "Sapphic: I Said to My Instrument," "Shot Messengers," and "The World" in *Explosive.*

"The Sky Drank In" in *Best American Poetry: 1997*, Scribners.

"The World," "The Masters," and "Beauty and the Beast" in *The Body Electric: Best Poems from the American Poetry Review, 1972-1999,* W.W. Norton.

"Love's Portfolio" in *jubilat.*

"Training Films of the Real" in *Influence and Mastery,* Paul Dry Books.

"Beauty and the Beast" in *Best Texas Writing 2,* Firewheel Editions.

Special thanks to Stefanie Marlis, Dale Going, and Domenic Stansberry. And to the Flute Girls.

Cover art: "Subterranean #1," Marie Carbone. Collage. 11" x 7 1/2" 1998.
Cover design by Ferenc Dobronyi
Typesetting by Kim Grant

The publication of this book is supported by a grant from the Pennsylvania Council on the Arts.

Library of Congress Control Number 00-132936
ISBN-0-88748-319-4
ISBN 0-88748-349-6 Pbk.

10 9 8 7 6 5 4 3 2 1

CONTENTS

In loving memory of Graham Gillis Conoley
February 27, 1919—July 20, 2000

What is a man who has outlived his God?

Herman Melville

Furthermore, there are an infinite number of worlds both like and unlike this world of ours. Atoms being infinite in number, as was proved already, are borne far out into space. For those atoms, which are of such nature that a world could be created out of them or made by them, have not been used up either on one world or on a limited number of worlds, nor again on the worlds that are alike, or on those which are different from these. So that there nowhere exists an obstacle to the infinite number of worlds.

Thomas Dumm

THE WORLD

It was just a gas station. It was not spectacular carnage.

A woman in the parking lot, red I Love Lucy kerchief, dousing his shirts with lighter fluid,

a great love and a paranormal morning.

In the far fields   the aliens arriving, switching off the ignition,

new crisp list of abductees   though the closest we get is the radio.

Cool gray summer morning the first heat making an aura.

Let light. She lights each panel. Fires twisting.

Whatever must seek out its partner and annihilate with it. A great love.

The expansion today is just a gas station. It is not spectacular carnage.

So one has a set of events from which one finds one can't escape

to reach a distant observer.   And a star is born.

Red giant, super giant, white dwarf.

We observe a large number of these white dwarf stars.

Giant Sirius, the brightest in the night sky,

dog star. What we could have been had not the star

been present, too much presence

seeping out of us— red the I Love Lucy kerchief draped over the lamp.

A she-ness to the table.   Pearls on the bread plate, make-up on the napkin,

a couple of burned-out butts.

(Alien intake valves?)

And come night: a supper club.

High risk behavior in cinemascopic rain.

The heat released in this reaction,

which is like, a controlled hydrogen bomb explosion,

which is like, what makes stars shine.

Boy Pegasus   Boy Mercury   Sister Venus

the stars so compulsively readable   the sun eight light minutes away,

Birthmark.   At the red end of the spectrum.

Three gold-jacketed overly friendly men smiling,

poling before the nymph of a red river   burning in the presence of the floor plans.

For the world is one world now   not that you may own your own home.

Sinter me, sister.   Threescore skullduggery,   endless cradle holding a space open.

Rufous skylark,   tell us off the skiff,

sun up, the next day,   we're looking into a box.

Let's see the world.   Are you coming with me.   What's for dinner.

SEVERAL SKYLINES

The city adored the roadmap

the pencil taken from my hair
a mall of fireflies, a lakefront of white noise.

Money is

no final resting place
no closed down factory

lit in the supple way
everything measured tries looking.

The sky produces tender

colors down the aisles
each promise

blurred, the boxed

slogans and bright hands
arrested
in the glare—

My headlines mildewed in the storm.
The pipe bomb extant in the abandoned truck,
and in the big pain of not having
a million things, of being alone and with free time,

there was no landscape,
no one way
to walk the highway.

I'm going out now with a towel and a cooler for the river.

I start and error, and am protected by music.
Where the future shatters
a tiny office,
where a sister dies her hair, and dies her hair, to show what silence really is.

CANON

In the *as if, as if*   of storm into soaked leaves

                                    the traffic's hiss
pantyhose on the clothes hanger

                a personal life written on newsprint

a beautiful acting out—

Later I deep-fried the catfish and let the grease drain.

On the screen's unwadded bedsheet,
the woman stabbed and the man running
about as long as a movie.
The moths born pile to hole in our towels.

As we put our books down
                            and took the stairs
and walked straight
to the stores,
            as we made out shapes

with respect   in kind
in deliverance   in ardor

(anxious red wagon beside the moving library)

as we wished, as we said, as we gave birth or not,
it all got uttered,

again   again

until whether in scale or in patina,
we began to drift away from the conversation like thought,

your flourish,

my balm and plumb,

(who was that speaking)

We must remember everything,   *everything*

palm from infinity broken

THE WORLD

It is honest.

It is most unfair.

A day consisting wholly of noises.

Unsuspecting people shooting a playground with guns.
Never caused

any trouble before. I don't get it. No matter whether

I buy the orange one, or the magenta, or the chartreuse,
I've gone west, and I feel tranquil, not elated.

Cold wet girl squealing on her slip-n-slide,

slow river of hypodermics under a street lamp, anonymous deaths and not so asinine.

White, yellow, black,

a space preceding the image and a space following,

space and waste and shadow,
and Kilroy was   and Kilroy was

garnets under a radiation apron,

the quantum figures figured out
then crumpled up

and tucked
under your windshield.

Memory a kind of faceless Amish doll shivering me timbers, dancing in crushed shoes.

Where I come here, rounding the corner in my new speedster, and I ask you.

No, the landscape is not a collage.   It is wholly original.   My bare hands.

TRAINING FILMS OF THE REAL

I.

Late shank of the evening: ligustrum pollen   on yellow walnut leaves,
two small girls   playing,   in sun,   young retinas   virtually empty

as: while pumping gas one sees   immaterial ones randomize rest stops,
as: in life,

black is,   blue is,   as in life   green becomes.
A red slashes

a red divides   white scallions   along a scaly riverbank.

A few new sprouts of cress   a crazed environmentalist
     shouting   *get off*.

As in life, I had meant the yellow
gaze of an ecstatic   over the unstainable industrial carpetting.

In the weedy old Victorian   sheltering the beakers, scales   of the meth lab,
oh yes   it's karmic   to print money.

Woman in creamy white slip   lacy bodice   a can of Colt 45
one finger fastening   the small rusty buckle of a strap.

May the baby wake.   Restoring respect   to the teamsters. Tremolo in the pipes
as cold and heat   trade places.

For the sound of a lute   out on water   she applies light makeup and sings,
Don't Explain.

II.

Teenagers xerox
genitalia.   Well that's a big if
what could they   *mean* by that

expanding moment
leaves falling
entire afternoon

                                    spent looking
at the inscrutable,

days,   days

each blind
poet
                        with magnifying glass over OED

                                                      akin

to Dostoevsky's
never,

no sound of the gun   to come ringing through   the ears,

nevermore,

nevermore,

Green

bottle of pills   scattering across   a tile floor

POW in a recliner   tuning his ear   to the choir of his camp

as winter   and spring   depart.

III.

For better feng shui
I'd eat a low stack of silver dollars.

The key to it all   dangling on the tool shed wall
within   a soda's reach.

The aliens   haruspicating overnight   my heart   spleen
which has   nothing to explain   to the chest cavity.

Nor to the forest's blondest wood.

If you have to   smooth grammar   to get clear,
—most imperial   royal model

bits of jade at her   clavicle—   may we
twin   the nouns,

may we twin   the whole experience
while   better demons   butter the downtown.

The wind tithes.
The wind

        tithes   and punctures   trying a piece of scenery.

People slow   to see the lights   across the pond.

May the time   come.   Loved,
unmocked conduit   stretching a whole figure   over the sundial.

May the jail cell   house   one's valuables   in the dell.

TURNED BACK

So hot at the filling station

everyone moving like the not quite

utterly dead, a youth sucking on a mint, a toddler kicking a can of pop,

someone taking the key to the "john" taking obvious pleasure

in becoming another one
                    of the unlocated—

You can read the mystics/ you can lay down with the martyrs

and brood
on that other
as one would fade in a river

beside infant white

                    foliage of the road

in the may-shine.

            Cloud's

thin amorphous plumage,

Daphne's singular girl peeking out from a tree
as time lags

            while the photos come back developed,

heavy beam of a head pressing down the frail summer leaves.

Inside the pumps the numbers rise,

and here a mind wanders here the fumes escape,   a youth walks out through the noon.

Someone rushes around
the cash register

        hands smoothing the money
        like an attention span—

the silver drawer a site of purity
                        a zero aperture

                        a youth's cigarette

                        stabbed into tawny scratches

on the wall, someone's

            unspelled misery over a plot of marigolds—

The silver drawer lowering with the cash

            where you step forward

eye seeking eye in the pyramid,
in the paper oiled

in strip mall's
        blunt shadow cooling the back of your neck,

identity falling through the shaft
        before finding another house-a-fire for you,

        (and through
        the lively opening)

whose both ways close
with the silence of those

whose power can no longer enter anywhere,

        the sun in the present,
that fame—

someone flipping the radio putting voice over abyss

        someone folding a map

        someone bringing the sunglasses back down.

IS THIS IRRITATING OR IS THIS A PLEASURE

Not experiencing one's whole life
as some aggravating interruption

In the yes/no opposition with which Buddhists like to irritate
and with that wry humor.

Many people doing the same thing period.

When one has no feeling for harmony.

Pear blossom blue and purple wisteria breeze   the politic
nailing something in   wind chime   leaf   taking time with its shadow

—windows scummy as though they'd gone through a day—

vetch vetch those flower sounds
seductive too,

and they punctuate
without one human thought.

What if there is not enough nothing?
The real black humor being that we'd filled it.

A naked I a fully clothed I
Culture is my hairshirt

Bad fruit
hanging there
rope tied and swung across
the horses slapped hard on the rear
so as to run away from the associations

Christ's splayed hand
truth's striking ease

What I mean is:
my funny valentine

What I mean is:
no evidence of mercy

THE SKY DRANK IN

The sky drank in   sparrows making lucid the oaks.   The leaves sank onto the stair.

And you   as you were,   I as I become, color and form, bend and start,   split one

on the other side of *the screen of*   *your projections*—

you wanted me.   But I wasn't around,   only a small soul asleep   in the high heel,

or fluttering among the cosmetics   blindly, usually just a pause   between

what's there and not there,   mail on the stoop,   lists   "to do"

and other narcotics   we call beauty,   symmetry, harmony,

and no supplied thing—   Only a weak-edged soul,   the almost seen

luminous circle breaking   to parenthesis,   tender embrace   trying to enclose

whether for an instant or an eternity,   something is

"true—"   The sky   drank in sparrows making lucid the oaks.   Whirl

of particles in the desire of   whatever I sought   when I began

these sentences   (I stay,   I have stayed, I am staying),

the slow burning in of the come on   darling, the salesman,   the waitress,

the couple fighting in the phone booth   heart wall to heart wall,

palm,   darkening lip,   the infinities that *were, were*

our mouths and our sex—   you who were not   becoming not again—

lovers   in the used world,   more extinguished, finer,

o you-again,   o one,   o no one,   o you—

THE VIOLENCE

We must try to rid evil of our character, the president says.

The president is paling, another mouth of extinction, suggested the Fox.

I said over here, goddamn it, and not in the garage. I was
fourteen,

and learning to drive,
I knew the beloved must not be a monster in the head.

And so, the world sins, it is exhausted, ministering to the misbegotten.

And so, shuttered in the subway, a murderer
rides between cars, so that he is before the wrong,
and the dead wrong, brother.

I was far from home. He held up a blank sign and I let him in the car. I did not want to
tarry.

My beloved is not
a monster in the head, my beloved is either
God's vengeance or his love,

entrails or insight,
I can only give you my word, though the fire in my eyes
is almost
his fire.

Genet: "A miracle is unclean: the peace I was searching for
        in the latrines and that I'm seeking
        in remembrance is a reassuring and silky peace."

Heraclitus: "Come in, there are Gods here, too.
        Don't be a stranger at the threshold."

In the tear of the pattern

no fleece shall cover you,
no seed-time, no unguent, no mystical birds, no eternal variant, gentian, algebraic,

no
eloquent
                alcohol, in the tear of the pattern,
no weed-grown

trail where a person could rest
in one
of a few mutilated copies—

Our no God sitting low on the other half of the tree, her shroud drawn over her hair—

Then take the cloth up again, the president says.

In the tear of the pattern, the wolf is whole, suggested the Fox.

And you are most vile.
You are a threshold spikily
gone through.

So this is your winter body, so this is your summer ass.

Sunlight glints over the breasts and the early evening newspaper, God's vengeance,
or his love,

whose voice
so lightly   come of wounds

who loves   this way—

HOW DO I

How do I

How do I
count when it was another kind of verdancy
that brought me to you—

the ways not knowing otherwise
the trees weighted into a kind of prayerfulness
the wildflowers standing up against us, against being, against ideal Grace

so that we may forego symmetry

so that passion finds use
in we left to count when the breath
is not a grief and is not for counting

but is this repetition and this eternity

how I do, even
in most quiet need

discount ever
my unblinking glance my open face

how do I, in the tentative sun
that comes into

the nonfading
of the there we sat, there we were, after death.

THE SPLENDOR FRAGMENTS

—

Between X and noon,
the blend of acids, sentiments, returning

weather which makes the night
transparent to think of—

like God's lonely imagination, and God's dark authority—

how for him
Death is the loving one, perfect for beating life into form.

—

"This way, please,"
was all she told me,

more her mouth   holding onto the words
than speaking,
        because no sound came out—
no melon patch on a summer's morn.

—

The words LIVE GIRLS torn
on the telephone pole, the earlier details
gone,

in country and in town.
Twilight. Forms
darkening,

how after the epidural
the hospital a shady white hotel.

—

A lonely rook strikes her beak
     against the white surface of the lake,

a pleasant drunkenness,
     a doubtful authorship.

—

In a climate of suspicion,
     fish fried, sheets hung,
          a rosebush

detonates,
     only what is in shadow

mattering
     truly, eternally.

—

As when Genji's lover
     covers her mouth to laugh,
and the powder comes off in her hands.

—

In the mall's
    vector of space

mannequins bent at the knees
    open eyes of longing

I tried on this dress,
a false pregnancy.

        —

       Summers in underpants,
       blue tangled shopping cart,
       everyone out for the immersion—

         like Stein
       composing *Three Lives*
             under that Matisse—

Pretty soon—
     pretty soon I caught the drift of God's speech

            before I polarized
     completely.

     Doggy in a window:

     little lamb   who   made   thee

—

    First sunny day
             after rain,
  my eyes just touched by the blue—

Visibility's   candidate, the mass marketers
enter me into their new computer,
           I wander freely

amid cars parked sideways
in brilliant rooms—

—

    Eternity flattens. And opens,

    like sitting alone for a moment in a cafe
    in a hole in the wall in the sorry chair in the middle of the dirt of the place,

        then the urge to take that look off your face,
        get the particular hell home.

———

The obduracy of spirit,
the loathing of self,
and the night, very fast—

on the overpass on our way to your house
I'm thinking new lover how well you speak my language

      taking the exit as we move beyond
the new sign,

      but blank this time—

                the saying coming down the road
                on a truck somewhere

                like a little white bible in the human mind

                all that absence of being on the freeway

           through the portholes (false manor) my hand grazes yours

                a fool flies

—

Above moving sidewalks,
in shrinking headspace, pressed

among others,
unboundaried hair skin familiar to the touch,

I caught a movement of God's
lips, begging the question,
but he wouldn't
speak—   you don't   love me?

—

My waterloo, my diorama.

A white cypress

stretches

a fair hand.

Interior sea,

smooth urban lake,

all its runners
                    drunk on fresh air

and syncopating their legs

left, right, breath,   no breath,

                    where shafts of the sun had fallen,

                    or as far as what's seen

                              (will stay)

34

THREE WOMEN THEN A STILL LIFE

Make a figure   of frequency   a figure living   a social struggle

a man   once   who grew   breasts   you could see them   especially

when   agititated in water   my toy bride   in so public   a gown

those aren't arms   they're gestures   that isn't   a drawbridge

that's   my   personality   May I fit   my arm   through   your arm,

so   proprioceptively   as when   one plays   some   instrument

one opens   a fan   the creek drain   while we turn away   and   creep now,

creep on all fours and   Turn   on the light   turn on   the light

her black paintings   her   zero-level   memoir   Oriole

says to Fox,   no matter   what you want   to say   about it,

we should   ink up   those   titties   In what sun   do the neurons   of the brain

bask   their ripe produce   as a function   of having to be   one   plays

Flag   go   hang   over action   separated   She was   once   a

once a   once a   in the   aborescent   fronds of summer

in the   instructions   the orchard   oriole   sang   of herself

life's curvatures   the cassettes   in   a coitus   full of   bursting

with   face   face of a human   three women   waist-deep in water

directing   white cattle

CHILDHOOD HOME, A PANORAMA

A crow on the telephone pole, tingeing daylight.

A television
in daylight
is a clear cosmetic bag,

is a transformation and a recreation,

a water in the inner ear.
A black woman is lowered
on a creaky Otis elevator—

originally designed for polio victims in the home—

a vacuum cleaner's hose wrapped around one ankle,
she raised me. I love her.

Will you pour me a sidewalk? she asks.

My sister a stripe of white above her black eyeliner
turning over out of her sunbath.

Surely a murder, surely a murder
places itself deep center, in the kitchen, in the hallway,

in the myrtle, in the purple vitex,
in the laughing that took you up tearing mint for the tea.

A Japanese soldier's sword hanging over the mantel,
sea pearls encrusted on the blood-splattered handle,

with no sense to the story at all,

like the sense of shape in a bowl of farm eggs,
their barely connecting

peripheries of humor.

Are you a handler, a healer, or an eater?

The eyes of strangers come to town in the right conditions
refracting red

in sulphur glow and pitchlight, the rattlesnakes obey
men without shirts,

silver buckles glinting over their blackened jeans.

Hot spectra
filling the falling summer sky,

somehow equivalent to leaving the next day without a trace.

In a loose white housedress a neighbor walks to the same crack
in the sidewalk every afternoon, and back. Cipher that.

As a practice I find it to be almost insatiable.

In the distance the lamentation of the train,
the lamentation of things no longer important.

What kind of facts began to hang in your brain?

Oxygenation, a mindful weather in the kitchen, half a melon.

The beds in their disheveled beauty.
Ever-biding sun.

We are glorious, but grow
in the awful knowledge that governors and heroes
rise in houses such as these.

A plaque that could say,
a plaque that could one day say a little history
to make you stop.

My sister handing me a training bra. My sister's eyes a hazel green.

On the side porch all the men I will ever kiss.
But not the women, and not the children.

No matter what, I will swear I didn't do it.

It's hot, it's hot, it's hot.

THE FIRST THREE MINUTES

Deathless galaxies,
our beds,
unmade—

My sister reaching over me.
My sister going up in flames.

Our growstick
next to a tenuous mirror.

And like not the thing itself
but the culture that produced it, the thing opening.

All the future things   (we would make the car red,
        the guitar acoustic, a clear day
            would be one without membrane—)

shaking out like that,
        with no one around, the early convulsing—

The system becoming system,
before we knew it, dicey stars and a weak radio static,

time misfiring into the embarrassing moments before no theory
could take us to,

the black night in the black night

and where was the signature

and where was the mop against the door—

LOVERS IN THE USED WORLD

A luna moth
          in night's friable matter,

spun right into the image shadow, spun

behind time,
in the erstwhile Nowhere,

where silence
sends word

they are living over the difficulty: that what got lost in the mutations
was not what was

lost in mutability,

the leaves in comfort, the leaves in error,

in the channels of time spiralling
in spent time:

            some rainy summer day with the sun out.

Her hair pinked, lifted
behind her, she is teasing myth's

trajectory in the sun-slatted tunnel where she can watch the heroines fly.

He is listing the summer words.

The *lucid* and *drowned* and *lost*,
and the "light" and the "fields" and the "huge"

and the thoughtful—

where they reach a space—
          like brides come to be annointed

in a vatic streak—

A white, white interior—

Matter dropping into its sinkholes
matter blowing off the visible stars

the motes of dust authoring

who among us

who among us
would live more fatefully

and not in just what
chance arranges—

And without hunger
for the way images become one and beauty scans the eye,

and girls scrape
the rocks weaving.

How then are we borne up?

The great hand smoothing over
the great hand smoothing over,

and lifted from the fire.

IN THE WIND THAT UNHANDS YOU

Our hearts no less carnal, and no less sitting loose from God.

Our hearts war in the leaves.
The end is sweet.

Between wind and calm,
an intimate vicinity—   a new air,

a lambent sideways rain extracted from the oaks.

And the light porous and changing,
                the pantyhose whose gesture summons ever,

while in stopped traffic
the black-suited evangelist

                who in his devotion

fastens us all upon this frame of hope:
images to end—

                Or how ultimately
                in a white bathing suit.

You were the glory of sitting in peace for a moment
before diving

right in—

                        (and discarding this, too.)

So you were the one
who found a cafe, who smoked, drank, read.

Who knew the details and procedures, the streets and films,
your legs apart,
the tense held.

Bare the square
and the unwavering elm,

       then the screens
               dropping down

with their products for what

           you are going through— One by one

       the images left you,
each folding away   like faces and litter—

At the airport   a lover's embrace,

then the cool air up
from the grate,

first the plenitude,

       then the vast emptiness left,

in relief   and not replaced,

       and for once not wanting

           another   beauty

SAPPHIC: I SAID TO MY INSTRUMENT

Chapeau in sky before the photographer

Bringing me up
upon thigh   this is much

To envisage like the spin of the yellow street sweeper going at it now

And if there were another
beseech you to tell me

Had I not brought that lingerie into the dusk

Had we not
discussed it further

I would go for you to divine me

The forest sans darkness
sans wet muddy tracks

Spaces necessary to depart
in one finger's revolution

The skin has little breathing room

Previously it would have behooved me to illustrate the night was far the day long

You were legions off and nigh

re: shirts left out on the bed
re: la luna in an old postcard

You had gone/come back to this golden panel

No nethering its blackbirds
you were drinking coffee

Head bent over red counter shoulders smoothed

In sphere's harmony   you were so at hotel with me

Taking your hands from under the spigot   you were offering me a Lucky

Every. Youth. Was.   There.

CAREFUL

Paper boat   the wind loaned.

This difficult manuevering under an umbrella
spokes of ribs,   I elbow you.

Peeping Tom of nothingness
catching a video of you

buying a pistol 10 days ago, wary of intruders.

Shot messengers
in day's fold,

green, a miner's lamp,
green, the aftershave.

In a roadside tavern, a reader crumpling a letter back into an envelope,   what if.

Thus I had carpentered our entire relationship to go upstream.

LOVE'S PORTFOLIO

A fragment
of a fair copy would undo our slant meeting,

an in-flight movie
where we chatted

how life was choosing not choosing.

Joy and gravitation,
the day turned

canonical,
                    my book's cover and spine.

The sky blued
vagrant scribblings into print culture,

what shall be clad,
            the day's whole cloth.

A scribal hand,
a something.

A kiss away,   a kiss away,   a reader's
curve,

                        a reader's little addict
in black pants who would like to

            sit in the dust as Heav'n's other spangles do.

I lowered
I wrote the answers on whose hand
I approached
as an alias, trachea
                    without sound,   my signature,   bright felon.

BEAUTY AND THE BEAST

That the transactions would end.

That the rose would open
        (her appearance in a Cyrillic blouse),

leaving the sense
that one had reached for it—

dust gray blue green manifold red and torn,
        his studied performance of a romantic mood.

He is still eating other small beasts.

She is sleeping alone
coiffed in the pleated moments,

only rising to bathe before the mirror
with its grand so what.

But we who have held the book with both hands
and let the syntax shape us

we are not evermore
as mirror or sleep.

In our modern cloven space
events dissolve to the sexual instant,

each of us holding the hairy hand
with thrilling lucidity.

So we never find out what we mean
but it flakes off on our hands,

so the pleasures we most desire
go unexpressed,

people of the future will also have

light, fragile conversation
and a hidden cottage with shutters carved,

where each summer we return
with no misgivings, no spectacle—

Nothing to be afraid of.

Only the 16th century air,
making it impossible to breathe more purely.

And she is femaling him.
And he is maling her.

And someone says, the end.
And someone says,

no, this is my body.

THE MASTERS

The photographs were yellow where Death is a bidden slow form splitting cells
though the day is tremor, open, a red tanager

glimpsed on the way to the hospital as in the foreign thriller a Burmese monk
draped in scarlet and seen once, twice, before slipping back into the forest.

I walk in in my body's healthy maze, all my heroines spent and exhausted,
all your masters assholes by now,

between existence and non, the humiliation of a hospital gown, the wide shoulders
as when we first met and I could hold you and not be defined

by the turmoil of I, sorry and afraid, a stale, tired radiance—

And so the ghosts of erotica wanting to know could they still
get a rise out of us, but we were just a space some others had their eyes on, unkept,

untried, our breath, our fumes—

A part of me was already standing at the pay phone.
A part of me was pressing against space,

I couldn't shape anything, the Fates in the corner hiking their skirts
as I helped you from bed, whose small, colorless laugh.

FUCK THE MILLENIUM

A photograph a beautiful woman

A photograph of a beautiful woman

Now that's it, hold it   right there,
would you just turn the head a little to the side

White cypresses, telephones dangling out of

my sorry images

Certain unsteady figure in raincoat watching
        her counter figure
cross the street carrying on completely normal life

so she's feeling constructed but still has to walk around

Unseen historical figures
belligerent with obscene greed

reacting metaphorical to what,

who is dominant?

Rot me, rot me, cry the birds
from the flowering compost

particle drawn to particle, o optical day

Certain figure in raincoat
crying now

everyone passing by trying to look away

Culture
invading a huge hole in the realism

Not to achieve a mere semblance

Marina Tsvetaeva

left hanging too long
as no one wanted to be seen

as connected to that

Standing alone as through the sun

tragedy is glory in an ideal mirror

Standing alone as through the sun cut in strips
no one sees us though we're watching

A beautiful woman photographing
a stand-off at the day-care center

A foiled bank robbery   made someone   shooting mad

Lipsticked on a banner: I don't want witness   I want cure

I held a good bird dying in my hand, archer

Let it be remembered I was linked with the use of the camera

SHOT MESSENGER

Post–eternal,   the season gliding.

Two cut   agapanthas,   *these are*

my greeting   home an entire   co–air,

all climate and no equator.

Continuous   last minute at the gate.

Planes let rivers with a flame,

where you throw your hat

is firmament.

It makes no sense to listen.

A toy ferris wheel,   a uniform.

I used   to.   I used.

Sky's folio:

A stranger turns: a way of dressing

FLUTE GIRL

I kept coming in whenever anyone else entered,
like the drunk man,

or behind
Socrates, a sudden opening

like quick grabbing an extra newspaper off
someone else's coin

      before the latch shuts,
or the soft hush of the ATM card as it enters—

these are sounds
you may know intimately.

Love a silver reed.
Between the teeth.

      Some words
creaked
coming out of the rhetoric—

I was sent away.
Back into the opening.
         The blur of the other side
where I'm hidden
     though not exactly

stricken,
              beautiful and silent so that I may be lacking—

This is
what made me

       audible to you.

ALCIBIADES

A boy at table   comes a man in cloak

a leg seems   a light discrete

a wrong door, a wrong door,   some wake

if he   had loved me   his talk would not have been

almost   the talk of a god

blankets between us   too earthly

breath   the off-green of new grapes

love   exchanging itself for words   is like

kissing your sister   kissing your older brother when you sleep

SOCRATES

Predictably Socrates is late to the seminar on Socrates.

He is too at hotel with himself,

a place in his voice no sound comes through,

opposite of evangelist.

Like a situation in his dreams in which he couldn't.

All this could happen,

even to Mr. For Whom the Birds Must Stop Singing.

For us, too, so a feeling is changing, and soon   it's cut here,

what dawn is this

      humans tumbling

and the star hanging

enchant   as neon interrupts to rose.

No one can know what is wanted.

Before it all starts flowing into a different emotion.

THE WORLD

Sweet nullity.

You had come back to this red counter　　with your thorny

everyman's hands　　you were drinking coffee

behind plate glass,　　a person experiencing a person's dimensions, a thousand-fold,

la luna in an old postcard.

Lesions etc., moon's tissue, etc.

Do not fix it in the eye—go!

Do not read it in the book—live!

Unrepeatable

as sky's folio:

The waitress's hands under the spigot　　you were offering me a Lucky

DATE MOVIE

How I had come to you,

how you had come to me,

the wind parting hair on the boulevard.
The night vendors,

the newspaper's blot,

the rain stopping into
the rape sheet and body tally

not the clean slate we crave,
our late bodies

worked into a fitness that keeps us like lambs fenced in a village,

in a "ruin of a culture," in a black rain—

The earth tilting
in apogee, or just like

       jackpot winnings,

we pray a good crosswind
gets us out of this barn place, that has no art.

So tell me how is it

Mary gets changed into a little girl in the arms of her son
who henceforth becomes her father—

and does this make her still
his mother, his daughter,

or his wife?

Thus a wanderlust began

preceding the specificity of us,

(as in anticipation of
as in the theatre now

                        the velvet curtains parting),

and we turned our faces to the larger faces, and grew
to resemble such conditions
in the night damp

until there was nothing left to look at—

Between watching
and being watched,

were we a welcomed sight,

like when money
was first pinned to the madonna, the first parade?

Between
seeing and believing,

I love the liquefaction of your voice.

A treble in the high wire shiver if
I get a recorded voice,

how if we let the lawn go natural,

the insects will return,
faint discordant American rhythms

in the offing.
Come in, please.

These plums are still warm from the sun and slightly pungent in the crab grass.

Over our nakedness,
a thrown blanket's disquieting

undertow of air.
A live color broadcast over the moon, red drape.

THE WORLD

Some are born
some are born

              selfhood marches

                         across the surface an owl lifts on bony wings

Whose brain
whose brain
          furnaced

the eyelash   the sparrow   the cat   the marguerite
the Floridas, the Mediterraneans,

o lawful bread
o wondrous portal

Here come our enlarged and nefarious senses

(a couple arguing old world
malarkey   under the honeyed streaks on–site

prestidigitous   platelets of cloud   floating past)

Here's a form
we need to fill in

                and hold lanterns and double space into

the password for
           how we found
           time to do it

time grainy and full   time mowing down

Some are born
some are born

silence throwing itself   asunder   spectre   joyous

Some are born

          who find use

          use some of this

          use this

NOTES

"Several Skylines" is for Donald Revell.

"The World," (the second poem of that title, on page 14) is for Sheryl Smith.

"The Sky Drank In": the phrase "the other side of the screen of your projections" is Luce Irigaray.

"How Do I" is a "cover" or recasting of Elizabeth Barrett Brownings' "How Do I Love Thee?"

"The Splendor Fragments": the phrase "no melon patch on a summer's morn" is from Haruki Murakami's *Hard-boiled Wonderland and the End of the World*.

"Three Women Then a Still Life" is for Stefanie Marlis. The title comes from a line by Norma Cole.

"Canon": The phrase "a beautiful acting out" is Sappho via T. Begley and Olga Broumas' *Sappho's Gymnasium*.

"Lovers in the Used World" is for Hawley Hussey and Cecil Schmidt.

"Love's Portfolio": "Heav'n's other spangles" is Robert Vaughn.

"Flute Girl" is for the Flute Girls.

"Date Movie": The phrase "barn place" is Willem de Kooning, from his essay "Content is a Glimpse." The italicized passage is a loose paraphrase and condensation of the ideas expressed in Julia Kristeva's essay, "Stabat Mater."

"Turned Back" is for James Tate and Dara Wier, and for the use of a warm study on a rainy afternoon.